The Ninja: The History and Legacy of Feudal Japan's Secret Agents

By Charles River Editors

Prince Hikaru Genji and a ninja

About Charles River Editors

Charles River Editors is a boutique digital publishing company, specializing in bringing history back to life with educational and engaging books on a wide range of topics. Keep up to date with our new and free offerings with this 5 second sign up on our weekly mailing list, and visit Our Kindle Author Page to see other recently published Kindle titles.

We make these books for you and always want to know our readers' opinions, so we encourage you to leave reviews and look forward to publishing new and exciting titles each week.

Introduction

A 19th century depiction of a ninja

"They travelled in disguise to other territories to judge the situation of the enemy, they would inveigle their way into the midst of the enemy to discover gaps, and enter enemy castles to set them on fire, and carried out assassinations, arriving in secret." - Hanawa Hokinoichi

To most people in the West, particularly the youth, the mere mention of Japan immediately evokes various images. A delectable rainbow of sushi, hand-rolled temaki, and platters of crispy, golden-brown tempura. An idyllic, crystal-clear lake flanked by trees covered with delicate, cotton-candy-pink sakura blossoms. A montage of unique, hand-drawn cartoons that are a masterful mix of delightfully exaggerated proportions, features, and colors, and elements of arresting realism, collectively known as "anime."

Then, of course, there's the ninja, a willowy, graceful figure decked out in black from head to toe, his glinting eyes peering out from the window of his balaclava. He flits from rooftop to rooftop in stunning somersaults and slinks into the shadows, watching his unsuspecting marks from afar and calculating their every move. Then, as quickly as he came, he strikes, hurling throwing stars, twirling his nunchucks, and hacking away with his trusty sword, exterminating his targets with dizzying, lightning-quick speed and superhuman precision. At least, this is how those unfamiliar with the ancient art of ninjutsu, or shinobi-jutsu, see them.

Ninjas are, without a doubt, one of the most timeless and far-reaching cultural staples ever to emerge from Japan. They have become a global phenomenon, and there are countless depictions of ninjas in comic books, films, TV shows, video games, toys, and other forms of popular culture around the world, not to mention their continued relevance as a "conventional" go-to Halloween costume. Kids across the world are intimately familiar with Teenage Mutant Ninja Turtles, Snake Eyes from the G.I. Joe franchise, Scorpion from Mortal Kombat, and Black Noir from The Boys. Ninjas have also been featured in a slew of other international movies and TV shows, among them the 1986 Filipino film *The Legend of Ninja-Kol*, the 2010 Norwegian film *Norwegian Ninja*, the 1982 Turkish film *Holy Sword*, and the 2002 New Zealand film *Tongan Ninja*.

The Ninja: The History and Legacy of Feudal Japan's Secret Agents looks at who the ninjas were, how they fought, and the events in which they played a leading part. Along with pictures of important people, places, and events, you will learn about the ninjas like never before.

The Ninja: The History and Legacy of Feudal Japan's Secret Agents

The Rise of the Ninja

"The bamboo that bends is stronger than the oak that resists." – Japanese proverb

Legend has it that ninjas, or "*shinobi*" as they were traditionally called, sprang from a mythical half-man, half-crow creature known as the "*Tengu*." They were originally portrayed as Buddhist antagonists and presented as villainous demons, but their characterization was toned down over the years, evolving from malicious beings to profoundly wise, yet impish spirits. By the time the Middle Ages rolled around, the *Tengu* was depicted as an ally of the proletarian revolution, fighting against the corruption and oppression inflicted by the upper echelons of society.

The *shinobi* were associated with two types of *Tengu*. There was the *Daitengu*, which had a towering, muscular humanoid body and face with torch-red flesh, an elongated, proboscis-like nose, razor-sharp talons, and great, leathery wings, often clad in a monk's robe. These strange beings resided in the fringes of wooded mountainous regions, mainly on Mount Kurama, situated a little less than 10 miles north of Kyoto. The *Daitengu* worshiped the great *Tengu* god Sojobo, who was supposedly equipped with "1,000 times the strength" of the average *Tengu*. Like Sojobo, the *Daitengu* was often seen wielding a *hauchiwa*, or a magical fan fashioned out of feathers; with a single swish of the fan, the *Daitengu* conjured up mighty winds, typhoons, and other natural disasters. Some believe that the *Daitengu* were Buddhist monks who had gone off the rails in their former lives.

Then, there was the *Kotengu,* or the *Karasu-tengu*, which was more avian than human in its appearance. The *Kotengu* was more petite than the *Daitengu*, and had the head and wings of a fierce black crow, coupled with the torso and limbs of a man; they, too, sported the attire of a Buddhist monk. These creatures were placed near the bottom of the *Tengu* hierarchy, and were believed to have been servants to the *Daitengu*.

As a whole, the *Tengu* were immensely powerful entities. Apart from being highly proficient in various forms of martial arts and *kuji-in* (magic), they were gifted with super-strength, the power of flight, the power of possession, and shape-shifting abilities. On occasion, they also served as messengers for Sojobo and other deities. Taking all this into account, it is not difficult to draw the many parallels between the *Tengu* and the ninja. In fact, the masks traditionally donned by ninjas were called "*tengu-gui*."

According to local folklore, humans were kidnapped by the *Tengu* on a regular basis. The wicked *Tengu* tortured their captives. The benevolent *Tengu*, on the other hand, took their abductees under their wings, and trained them in *kuji-in*, a variety of combat skills, and numerous other special abilities. These humans were said to have been the world's first *shinobi*. The peasant folk captured by the *Tengu* during medieval times, as mentioned previously, were purportedly coached to incite a rebellion against their feudal overlords – namely, the samurais, *daimyo*, and the ruling shogunate.

A kindred folktale identifies the fabled Commander Minamoto no Yoshitsune as the world's first-ever ninja. Yoshitsune's early life was rife with tragedy. Not long after his first birthday, his father, who was the head of the Minamoto tribe, and his two eldest brothers were slain by the rival Taira tribe in the month-long Heiji Rebellion of 1160, wherein the aforementioned clans, subjects of Emperor Go-Shirakawa, locked horns over political power. Yoshitsune's quick-thinking mother whisked him off to an obscure village, where they found refuge for a few years; his half-brother, Yorimoto, however, was exiled to the Izu Province.

At the age of 10, Yoshitsune's mother consigned him to the custody of the monks at Kurama Temple – a monastery with a red exterior and a slate-blue hip-and-gable roof tucked away in Mount Kurama. It was here that child fell under the tutelage of the resident monks and in-house *Tengu*, or in other accounts, by Sojobo himself, who taught him a number of fighting techniques. He became particularly adept with his sword, and by his own account, perfected the skill of "flight." One of his primary instructors was an elderly abbot – or perhaps a *Tengu* in human form – by the name of Kiichi Hogen, a self-taught sage well-versed in the arcane secrets of the yin-and-yang, which he had absorbed from a sacred manuscript in his possession. Hogen's subordinates were forbidden from going anywhere near the precious codex, but Yoshitsune claimed to have devoured and memorized the material in its entirety by charming Hogen's daughter, who was apparently besotted with him.

The *shinobi* have also been linked to a mystical figure named En no Gyoja, or "En the Ascetic," whose life and works have been recounted in several books such as *Nihon ryoiki* (820), as well as his own biography, titled *En no Gyoja hongi* (724). Gyoja was born Kamo no Kozumi in Katsuragi of the Nara Prefecture circa 634 to a well-respected family of Shinto priests. Troubled by his fellow devotees' interpretation of Shintoism, Gyoja renounced his possessions and the comforts of village life, and relocated to a mountain cave in the south, where he pursued a life of rigid austerity and intense piety for over three decades.

It was during this period of extreme self-devotion and isolation that he allegedly acquired the esoteric knowledge and magical powers of Kujaku Myo-O, the Buddhist Peacock Wisdom King. He thus founded his own religion, which he dubbed "Shugendo," or "the path of training to achieve spiritual powers and longevity." This was essentially a cult of worship that featured a blend of asceticism, pre-sectarian Buddhism, animism, shamanism, Yin-Yang mysticism, elements of Taoism, Tantric Buddhism, and Kannabi Shinko practices, which revolved around the concept that mountains were the posthumous homes of human and agricultural spirits. The myth of the *Tengu* is thought to have been a product of the Shugendo religion.

The meditative practices, philosophical beliefs, and spiritual bond with nature, as well as the "magical" abilities of the incoming generation of medieval ninjas were rooted in Shugendo beliefs. The supernatural gifts attributed to Gyoja, which included shapeshifting on command – Gyoja's spirit animal being the ferocious and agile tiger – the ability to tread water, and the power to live on air and mist, are often incorporated into *shinobi* myth. Shugendo monks also underwent rigorous self-preservation training similar to those practiced by ninjas, among them tests of endurance wherein said monks were exposed to snow and frigid temperatures, and submerged waist-deep in icy-cold lakes, oftentimes under chilling waterfalls, for hours or days on end. Moreover, disciples claim that Gyoja's life was peppered with assassination attempts – all of which he inexplicably survived. Every sword or ax that struck Gyoja's shatterproof head, they say, always crumbled into pieces. This apparent invincibility is yet another trait often woven into ninja lore.

As fascinating as the ninja's *Tengu* and Shugendo roots may be, these are still widely considered to be no more than colorful myths (though the second and third tales are sprinkled with elements of truth). Nevertheless, the real history of the ninja is equally, if not more compelling.

The term "ninja" is believed to be a derivative of the characters 忍者, pronounced in *on'yomi* as "nin-sha." This is the Chinese pronunciation of the kanji (a Japanese writing system that uses adopted logographic Chinese symbols), while the word "*shinobi*" is merely the *kun'yomi* (the Japanese pronunciation of the kanji) reading of these symbols. It is uncertain whether these words preceded or succeeded the interchangeable terms "*ninjutsu*" or "*shinobi-jutsu*," meaning "the art of stealth, camouflage, and sabotage," a school of martial arts developed in feudal Japan. If the latter is true, the words "ninja" and "*shinobi*" may have simply stemmed from the names of this martial artform.

The older of the two words, *shinobi*, made one of its first appearances in writing in an 8th century poetry anthology – the first of its kind in Japan – titled *Man'yoshu*, or in English, *Collection of 10,000 Leaves*. This consisted of a whopping 4,496 poems. The word "*shinobikanetsumo*" was featured only once throughout the compilation in a short *waka* (poem) labeled "352-3," penned by a Lady Heguri. It was not a reference to an actual ninja, but a poetic descriptor for a silent, secretive (*shinobi*) individual (*mono*).

The word *shinobi* was only one of many words used to describe these unorthodox warriors, which varied by region. Such substitutes included *rappa,* meaning "ruffian"; *kusa,* meaning "grass"; *suppa,* meaning "spy" or thief"; *monomi,* meaning "one who sees"; *nokizaru,* meaning "macaque on the roof"; *kamari,* meaning "scouts"; and *onmitsu,* meaning "conceal" or "hide." The word "ninja" only became mainstream, especially in the Western world, in the mid-20th century, as foreigners deemed the word catchier and found that it rolled off the tongue more easily.

Authentic historical records regarding the first real-life ninjas, perhaps unsurprisingly, are few and far between. While it is known that *shinobi* culture entered its golden age in the 15th and 16th centuries, the precise origins of the ninja are still a matter of debate amongst chroniclers and experts. Ninja aficionados have concluded that the *shinobi* were in many cases deliberately excluded from the annals. British historian and prolific author Stephen Turnbull wrote in *Ninja AD 1460-1650*, "Ninjas...were invariably despised because of the contrast their ways presented to the samurai code of behavior. This may be partly due to the fact that many ninja [were from] the lower social classes, and that their secretive and underhand methods were the exact opposite of the ideals of the noble samurai facing squarely on to his enemy."

The first possible historical account of the ninja dates back to antiquity and is a thrilling tale chronicled in the *Kojiki* (712), the *Hitachi Fudoki* (718), and the *Nihoshoki* (720). Prince Yamato Takeru was the second son of Emperor Keiko, who was the 12th descendant of Jimmu, the founder of the Japanese dynasty. Often hailed as the "father of the ninjas," Takeru is believed to have been the first to utilize martial arts and espionage tactics in his missions.

In the winter of 397, 16-year-old Takeru had been tasked with assassinating Torishi-kaya and his younger brother, the two chiefs of the Kumaso clan. The Kumaso clan was a rebellious tribe based in what is now Kumamoto-ken in Kyushu, and it was actively revolting against Emperor Keiko's administration. Before infiltrating the Kumaso lair, Takeru slipped on a stunning, cerulean silk robe decorated with lace-white flowers, cinched at the waist with a ruby-red sash that had been gifted to him by his aunt, Princess Yamato Hime. He then styled in his hair in a half-up top-knot, held in place by the bejeweled comb of his wife Princess Otatchibana, allowing the rest of his glossy jet-black tresses to cascade down his back. He further ornamented his neck with garlands of vibrant jewels and beads, and with that, his transformation into a bewitching maiden was complete.

A depiction of Takeru in his disguise

  Cloaked in his disguise, Takeru entered the Kumaso headquarters in Southern Island. Torishi-kaya was instantly captivated by the ravishing enchantress and arranged for a banquet to be held in her honor later that evening. When the time came, Takeru continued to dazzle the brothers with her seductive charms and plied them with food and wine. As soon as the brothers, languorous and inebriated, lowered their guards, Takeru withdrew a grass-cleaving sword, the blade of Murakumo, hidden in his bosom, and plunged it into Torishi-kaya's chest. Startled, Torishi-kaya's younger brother scrambled towards the door, but the fleet-footed Takeru swooped down on him and stabbed him in his buttocks. Takeru then snuck out the rear entrance, hacked away at the blazing thicket of shrubs outside the palace after they had been set alight by the chiefs' minions, and vanished into the night undetected and unscathed.

  Another historical character frequently touted as the "father of the ninjas" is a 6th century operative named Otomono Sahito, who was at the service of Prince Shotoku Taishi of the Yamoto imperial family. Sahito has been credited with, under the orders of Prince Taishi, developing Japan's first sophisticated spy ring, the agents of which were referred to as "*shinobi*."

Not only was Sahito a veteran practitioner of numerous martial arts, he was a master of cloak-and-dagger techniques and reconnaissance, so much so that Taishi could "hear the words of 10 people at once."

However, while both Takeru and Sahito were referenced in multiple historical chronicles, historians remain doubtful as to whether these characters actually executed these awe-inspiring feats, or if certain details of their accomplishments were embellished for effect, as was custom at the time, given the lack of concrete evidence.

Hasetsukabe no Koharumaru, also known as the "Boy Spy," is yet another potential progenitor of medieval *shinobi* culture. *Shomonki*, an epic produced in 940, roughly midway into the Heian period, tells of the bitter dispute between a provincial magnate and samurai Taira no Masakado, and his warlord uncle Taira no Yoshikane. Initially, Masakado's men proved to be no match for the resourceful Yoshikane and his seasoned soldiers and suffered one humiliating defeat after another. Masakado, however, eventually succeeded in turning the tide, and launched a violent, wide-scale ambush that crippled Yoshikane's unsuspecting troops. Alienated from what was left of his comrades, Yoshikane had no choice but to fly the coop.

Disheartened but undeterred, Yoshikane planned his next move whilst laying low in his foxhole. About a week or so later, one of Yoshikane's contacts introduced him to a young fellow surnamed Koharumaru, a freelance messenger who occasionally worked for Masakado. Masakado sent for Koharumaru on January 22nd, 938, and presented him with an attractive proposition. Should Koharumaru agree to assist him in hatching a plot to vanquish his nephew once and for all, the penniless boy would be compensated with "mounds of rice" and several articles of new clothing, along with a guaranteed, permanent position as a spy in his employ, which came with a hefty salary. Koharumaru eagerly accepted Yoshikane's proposal.

As per Yoshikane's instructions, Koharumaru and another farmhand the warlord recruited posed as charcoal peddlers and began to stake out Masakado's estate. Masakado's personnel paid no mind to the spies, who proceeded to gather intel regarding the number of sentries patrolling the premises and the kinds of weapons stored in the armory, and even managed to produce a sketch of the layout within Masakado's residence. With this invaluable information at hand, Yoshikane assembled a crew and instigated a late-night raid on Masakado's estate.

Lo and behold, one of Masakado's guards had cottoned onto Yoshikane's scheme, who then promptly informed his master about the impending attack. Masakado immediately fortified his estate and succeeded in staving off the attackers. When Koharumaru learned of the failed ambush, he hastily packed up his belongings and fled for the hills. Unfortunately, he was waylaid by Masakado's men less than a fortnight later, who branded him a traitor and beheaded him for betraying his former master.

The story of Koharumaru serves as a prime example of the notoriety associated with traditional ninjas, who were perceived as unscrupulous, disloyal, and despicable individuals who flouted the *bushido* code upheld by honorable samurais. That said, some historians contend that these blanket judgments pertaining to the fickle and avaricious nature of the ninja are uncalled for. Though many of the *shinobi* were indeed free agents trained in espionage and counter-intelligence, Antony Cummins, founder of the Ninjutsu Research team, noted that "their place within the Japanese army was clearly understood."

The Way of the Ninja

"The first priority of the ninja is to win without fighting." – attributed to Maasaki Hatsumi, Grandmaster of the Togakure-ryu

The first school dedicated to *ninjutsu* was called the *"Togakure-ryu,"* or "The School of the Hidden Door," which was established towards the final years of the Heian period, more specifically the Juei era. The avant-garde academy was co-founded by a Shugendo elder named Kagakure Doshi (also referred to as "Kain Doshi") and his disciple, a defrocked samurai from Tokagure village named Daisuke Nishina whose once impeccable reputation was sullied in 1182 when his liege General Minamoto no Yoshinaka occupied the capital of Kyoto. Sadly, Yoshinaka's conquest was short-lived, for his cousin, the same Commander Yoshitsune mentioned above, unraveled his efforts with a successful counterattack. Yoshinaka subsequently perished when, upon recklessly crossing a frozen rice paddy on horseback, the ice underneath him disintegrated and swallowed him whole. Instead of committing *seppuku*, as was the norm for those in his line of work, Nishina, severely injured, staggered into the nearby woods and took cover until Yoshitsune's troops cleared off. Doshi stumbled upon the wounded samurai shortly thereafter and carried him off to his sanctuary in the Iga mountains.

A picture of the Iga mountains

Nishina later renamed himself "Daisuke Togakure" and designated himself as the Soke (grandmaster) of the *Togakure-ryu*, thereby laying the foundations for the rise of the first official generation of *shinobi* and simultaneously the first-ever ninja clan in Japan. Formally known as the "Iga Tribe," they would become one of the two most prominent ninja clans in the empire, the other being the Koga Clan (more on them later).

Yoshitsune, who secured the throne following the surrender of Yoshinaka's troops, was eventually ousted by his half-brother Yoritomo. Yoshitsune escaped by the skin of his teeth and sometime afterward erected the *Yoshitsune-ryu* of ninjutsu. Unlike Nishina's time-hallowed academy, however, Yoshitsune's *shinobi* training center, like many other similar institutions that cropped up in the following decades, failed to stand the test of time.

Contrary to popular belief, ninjas – at least, those who subscribed to Nishina's teachings – did not take pleasure in violence, nor revenge, and sought to steer clear of such actions at all costs if possible. Only when danger befell their country, their loved ones, or themselves did they resort to utilizing their combat skills. Their approach to this necessary evil was encapsulated in the following mantras: "Use the sword to be peaceful, and protect country, family, and nature" and "Embrace peaceful harmony with the same effortless compassion as that of the wildflowers."

Nishina's curriculum was comprised of 18 forms of *budo* ("the way of the war"), among which included: *Seishin Teiki Kyoyo* (spiritual refinement), *Taijutsu* (unarmed combat), *Cho-ho* (espionage), *Shinobi-iri* (infiltration by stealth) *Kenpo* (swordsmanship), *Yari* (spear-fighting), *Bajutsu* (horsemanship), *Bojutsu* (staff-fighting), *Suiren* (swimming), and *Henso-jutsu* (the art of disguise). Students were also trained in *Tonko-no-Jutsu,* or "the 12 forms of escape), and various *Karuwaza* crafts, a general term for *ninjutsu* acrobatics, such as the *Oten* (cartwheel), *Koho-tombogaeri* (back somersault against an opponent), *Zenpo-tenkai* (forward handspring), and *Shoten* (wall-running).

Only upon advancing to a certain rank were the Three Secrets, or the *Sanpo Hiden*, disclosed to the disciple. The secrets in question were the primary weapons of the Iga ninjas: the *Senban Shuriken,* a special four-pointed throwing star shaped like a diamond with a square-shaped hole in its center, a design unique to the *Togakure shinobi*; the *Shindake*, a thin bamboo tube measuring about 4-ft in length, used as an underwater breathing apparatus, as well as a blowgun; and the *Tekagi-shuko*, essentially four claw-like spikes attached to a metal device, which were then fitted over one's hand and fastened with leather straps, used as a climbing aid. The *Tetsubishi* was another weapon commonly attributed to the Togakure ninjas, which was their take on the caltrop; these were small objects with nine spiked points, reminiscent of the jacks used in games of knucklebones, that were at times, used as a *shuriken* alternative, and at times scattered across the road to puncture passing hooves and wheels.

Shinobi culture continued to develop quietly behind the scenes, gaining gradual, yet steady traction in the following century. Ninjas only returned to the limelight in the 1300s, as documented by the 40-chapter epic *Taiheiki* (Chronicle of Great Peace). The term "*shinobi*," used in the modern sense of the word, makes copious appearances throughout the *Taiheiki,* which is based on the *Nanboku-cho*: a turbulent period of conflict between the Northern Court of Shogun Ashikaga Takauji in Kyoto and Emperor Go-Daigo's Southern Court in Yoshino. One such example can be seen in the following excerpt from Chapter 20: "One night, as it was windy and raining, Moronao took advantage of the weather and sent out an *itsu mono-no-shinobi* (an excellent ninja) to infiltrate Hatchiman Yama and to set fire to the buildings."

The *shinobi* were also referenced in Chapter 24: "The shogunate's military governor, Tsuzuki-nyudo, led 200 armed people on a night raid, and approached Shijomibu from the direction where *kukkyo-no-shinobi* (robust ninjas) were hiding. These [*shinobi*] in the complex did not care for life or death and went to the top of a building, and after spending all their arrows, committed suicide."

Historians presume that ninjas were also involved in some capacity in the Onin-Bunmei War — a decade-long civil war beginning in 1467, which resulted from a feud over the heir of Shogun Ashikaga Yoshimasa. With 270,000 soldiers pitted against each another, this was the largest and deadliest battle in Japanese history, and as it happened, the Onin War was the very conflict that ushered in the Sengoku era, otherwise known as the "Warring States Period."

Although the extent of the *shinobi's* involvement in the Onin-Bunmei War remain a matter of speculation, chroniclers are positive that ninjas began to proliferate and were at their absolute prime during the Sengoku period, which has also been nicknamed the "Golden Age of the Ninja." This was an especially tempestuous time marked by chaos, anarchy, and frenzied infighting, particularly among the Daimyos, who were constantly crossing swords, both figuratively and literally, over territorial claims. As such, the demand for covert operatives – in other words, ninjas – skyrocketed. The *shinobi* of the Sengoku period undertook an array of roles, serving as spies, scouts, hired guns, pillagers, saboteurs, agitators, arsonists, and at times, all of the above. In a way, the ninja was viewed as the antithesis of the samurai, as the code of the latter warrior barred them from engaging in espionage, sabotage, seduction, and other "underhanded," stealth-related activities.

Naturally, the extensive market for these secret agents gave rise to a new breed of ninjas: the lesser-known female *shinobi*, otherwise referred to as the "*kunoichi*." Etymologists have yet to come to a consensus about the term's origins, but most believe that *kunoichi*, which translates to "nine plus one," was a crude biological reference to the 10 holes in women's' bodies, as opposed to the nine that men possess. While female ninjutsu practitioners were much rarer than their male counterparts, their existence is uncontested, and is cited across multiple historical records, such as the 17th century *shinobi* manual *Bansen-shukai*. Throughout history, and even in the present day, women tended to be overlooked and grossly underestimated, but it was precisely this gender discrimination that allowed the *kunoichi* to thrive, which they spun to their favor.

The *kunoichi* underwent the same grueling training as their male equivalents and were equally adroit at martial arts, and yet, they were seldom made to exercise their combat skills on the job. Instead, most *kunoichi* were handed surveillance-related assignments, often impersonating geishas, maids, and priestesses, and eavesdropping on war room meetings and the casual conversations of the enemy's staff, then relaying this classified information to their employers.

The *kunoichi* were also cast as "honey-traps," thereby using their sex appeal, as well as the act itself, as their primary weapons. It was common practice for *ryus* to dispatch scouts to various villages, where they were tasked with recruiting the most beautiful maidens, who were to be trained specifically for this purpose. There were different types of honey-trap missions. At times, they were commissioned to engage in one-night stands, but sometimes the job required them to play the long-con, which lasted anywhere between months to several years, in which they were instructed to masquerade as the enemy's mistress. When it came time to strike, the *kunoichi* would request a leave of absence, citing a desire to visit family. They returned days later with special suitcases outfitted with false bottoms. A male colleague lay in wait in this secret compartment. When the time was right, they exited their hideaway and penetrated the enemy lair as soon as the coast was clear.

Occasionally, a *kunoichi* was entrusted with carrying out assassinations. Still, the killing methods they employed were almost always passive, mainly death by poison, which were stored in vials hidden up their sleeves. They also utilized weapons specially tailored for the *kunoichi*. One of the most common *kunoichi* gadgets was the *neko-te*, which were a set of 1-3 inch talon-like nails affixed to stubby leather sleeves. The *kunoichi* slipped the *neko-te* onto their fingertips, oftentimes dipped in lethal venom beforehand, and pierced their "claws" into the target's neck. The *neko-te* were sometimes swapped out for modified hairpins sharpened to a point. Another *kunoichi* device was the *tessen,* or innocent-looking folding fans made with metal blades.

Like other traditional warriors, the *shinobi* adhered to their own pecking order, in which ranks and responsibilities were clearly defined. Not only was a power structure necessary for the effective execution of missions, this system enabled the *shinobi* to better safeguard their identities. Low-level ninjas never made direct contact with those on the top of the chain of command. If a mission went pear-shaped, low-level ninjas ensnared by the enemy would be unable to produce the names and whereabouts of their upper-level colleagues, which allowed the rest of the team to regroup and devise a different plan unimpeded.

These hierarchies varied by guild and clan, but for the most part, were split into three ranks. Seated at the top of the pyramid was the *jonin,* or "shonin," which loosely translates to "upper person." Despite their lofty titles, the *jonin* status was not exclusive to affluent, land-owning *daimyo*; chiefs of modest villages were also known to hold these posts. The *jonin* were in charge of formulating schemes, appointing *shinobi* to subordinate posts, and delegating missions and tasks, among other big-picture decision-making.

The "*genin*" were the lowest-level ninjas, equivalent to field operatives, who, when called into action, were ready to cast aside their daily duties at the drop of a hat. There were two sub-classes within the *genin* rank: the *yonin* and the *innin.* The *yonin* were the more educated *shinobi*, who handled surveillance, reconnaissance, and counter-espionage, whereas the *innin* dealt with more labor-intensive work.

Sandwiched between the *jonin* and the *genin* was the *chunin* or "*chujin,*" meaning "middleman." They served as the *jonin*'s right-hand man, as well as the liaison between the *jonin* and the *genin.* Once the *chunin* was thoroughly primed on the mission details by their superior, they rifled through the metaphorical *genin* roster and selected the *shinobi* most qualified for the task. The burdens of coordinating meetings, overseeing contracts, and other administrative protocols also fell upon their shoulders.

To the untrained eye, the differences between the layouts of a *shinobi* colony and a typical agricultural village were almost indistinguishable. Similar to the run-of-the-mill village, a *shinobi* settlement featured at least one temple, complete with a shrine and cemetery. The *jonin's* residence, along with those of other elders, would be located in the heart of the hamlet and encircled by a labyrinthine network of rice fields, which also doubled as moats, along with winding, sturdy bamboo fences or rows of thorny hedges. These were not elaborate, flamboyantly decorated shelters, as such structures were prone to attracting unwanted attention. Quite the opposite, the *jonin* resided in humble wooden dwellings that were only slightly more spacious than the average farmhouse. *Shinobi* settlements were also home to an assortment of rustic miniature castles, which served as offices of sorts for the ninjas. Their decision to spread out their bases was a strategic one; if one of their castles were breached, the *shinobi* could still fall back on the weapons and resources stashed away in their other forts.

In accordance with the *shinobi* hierarchy, the *chunin's* house was positioned a few blocks away from the *jonin's* residence and was shielded by similar barriers. The homes of the *genin*, who were often deemed expendable, dotted the periphery just behind the village's defensive walls. This allowed them to monitor the perimeter and man the watchtowers, which were furnished with bells. A series of smoke beacons were also installed on neighboring hilltops, which were ignited to warn the others about approaching enemies.

The exterior of a *shinobi* residence was intentionally designed to be inconspicuous and bore the appearance of a standard one-floor farmhouse topped with a chunky straw-thatched roof. More often than not, however, these were actually three-story structures with an invisible mezzanine and underground passages. Furthermore, these shelters were rigged from top to bottom with booby traps, such as false staircases that led to dead-end walls or spike-covered pits. Ninja homes were also tricked out with rotating walls; false floorboards that served as coffers for weapons, secret documents, and other valuables; trapdoors; and legitimate hidden staircases posing as bookcases and cupboards from which they could make a quick escape.

The *Ninpo* was to the *shinobi* what the *Bushido* was to the samurai, meaning it was an unofficial constitution that determined the ninja's conduct and ethics. Typically, these rules were never put on paper, but were instead orally passed on from one generation to the next, so as to ensure that their teachings and secrets were kept within the community.

As noted earlier, the *shinobi* were not violent by nature, nor were they invariably programmed to seek out material wealth. Their code was built upon the core principles of benevolence, courage, loyalty to their *sensei* (teachers and masters), duty, righteousness, honesty, and adaptability. The virtue of adaptability was a particularly vital quality to possess, particularly when performing a mission. Considering the high-pressure and unpredictable nature of the job, ninjas were encouraged to abandon conventional tactics and improvise on the spot, should the situation call for it. Ninjas were also taught to avoid the "three diseases" of *ninjutsu*: fear, trivializing an enemy's abilities, and overthinking.

The following were the 10 ninja ideals, as listed by the *Bansen-shukai*:

To maintain a strong body, with loyalty, bravery, strategem, skills, and belief.

To be gentle and faithful with less desire, to value academies, [and] to remember obligations.

To be eloquent, to read domestic and foreign books, [and] to be wise enough not to be cheated by anyone.

To know providence, to master the teachings of Buddhism and Confucianism, and to realize one's destiny.

To respect ancient, domestic, and foreign ethos, [and] to wear an equable temper.

To be called a good man, and to avoid arguments.

To maintain a decent household, to have a healthy, close-knit family, [and] never to betray anyone or abuse *ninjutsu*.

To travel around all countries, and to know the customs and manners of each land well.

To have a talent for literature, to excel in writing, [and] to possess a talent for and keen understanding of military affairs.

To acquire artistic talents like singing and dancing, traditional Japanese music, making impressions of others, and to utilize them when necessary.

For later generations, *shinobi-ism* was not an occupation that they readily chose; instead, it was one they inherited. Generally speaking, medieval civilians did not have the privilege of choosing their own romantic partners and had practically no control over their futures. The same applied to the *shinobi*, who were, at the end of the day, civilians first. Matchmaking was usually a job reserved for the ninja's *sensei*. Ninjas whose partners were infertile were constrained to adopt orphaned boys, for it was their duty to pass the *shinobi* ways unto their sons, who began their training as soon as they could walk, so as to expand upon the ninja reserve force. There was also a tactical aspect to *shinobi* marriages. Ninjas were stereotyped as lone wolves; therefore, the identity of a *shinobi* with a wife and children was far less likely to be fingered.

Given the absence of a stable currency system, ninjas of the Sengoku period did not receive a fixed monetary salary. The *shinobi* were often presented with silk, rice, and other prized commodities in return for their services. Most ninjas, especially those who resided in mountain villages preferred this mode of compensation, as old-fashioned agricultural communities, which relied on bartering, had little use for money.

Monetary compensation only became more prevalent in the Edo period. Although there was no going rate for ninjas, which was dependent on the guild and the class of mission they were assigned, there are a few historical accounts that allow for a peek into their wages. In 1582, Tokugawa Ieyasu forked over 1,000 kans (approximately $1 million today) to cover the wages of 200 ninjas for a single job, which works out to some 5 kans apiece ($5,000). Another account estimates that a *shinobi* who worked throughout the year could pull in an average of 36 kans ($36,000) per annum, which was a much more modest sum when compared to the yearly salary of a samurai. Ninjas entrusted with major missions were occasionally awarded a bonus, but large-scale assignments became increasingly scarce during the period of peace that succeeded the Warring States era, which undoubtedly resulted in steadily shrinking salaries. As such, most medieval ninjas had day jobs.

Training, Weapons, and Tools

"The way of the martial artist is the way of enduring, surviving, and prevailing over all that would destroy him. More than delivering strikes and slashes, and deeper in significance than the simple outwitting of an enemy, Ninpo is the way of attaining that which we need while making the world a better place. The skill of the Ninja is the art of winning." – Toshitsugu Takamatsu, the "last combat ninja" of the Bujinkan

Naturally, the amount and kinds of training that ninjas received were determined by their *sensei*, but all training programs, which were unequivocally strenuous and uncompromisingly stringent to say the least, encompassed the same fundamental drills and disciplines. Old-timers trained every bit as hard as novices, if not harder, considering their advanced ages, in order to maintain their physiques and to keep their mental dexterity and skill sets intact.

Solid survival instincts, situational awareness, and resilience were some of the most indispensable assets that a *shinobi* could acquire. In addition to braving extreme elements and depriving themselves of food and water for several days in a row, they walked, sprinted (forwards, backwards, and sideways), and swam great distances without pause. Ninjas were made to master a miscellany of walking styles, including: *Shinobi-ashi,* or "quiet feet," taking toe-to-heel steps; *Uki-ashi,* or "floating feet," meaning to walk *only* on one's tiptoes; *Yoko-bashiri,* or "the sideways walk," which was to flatten one's back against a wall, splay out one's limbs like a starfish, and walk from side to side; *Inubashiri,* or "dog-running," to move on all fours as necessitated by confined spaces with low ceilings; *Kitsune-bashiri*, or "fox-running," similar to dog-running, but on one's fingertips and tiptoes; and lastly, the most complex maneuver of them all: *Shinso Usagi-aruki,* also known as "deep-grass rabbit-walking," wherein one stifled the sounds of their footsteps completely by walking on their palms face-down.

Obviously, ninjas utilized their sprinting prowess to attack opponents and to flee from danger, but it also allowed them to convey information to their comrades or masters as quickly as possible. A renowned *shinobi* known only as "Idaten" reportedly ran an average of 124-miles a day.

Ninjas also camped out in different terrains, and they meticulously surveyed and studied the topographies of these environments. They learned how to find or construct their own shelters from scratch, how to hunt and gather edible plants, and how to identify special herbs that could be used to concoct medicinal potions. They also familiarized themselves with the basics of weather forecasting and taught themselves how to cobble together makeshift casts and tourniquets.

Shinobi training exercises were unlike any other. To start with, they scurried up walls and extremely steep inclines with ropes, foldable ladders, the *Tekagi-shuko,* and other similar equipment. Comparable to medieval parkour, ninjas vaulted over moats and leapt from one roof to another, among other obstacles spaced an average of 7-ft apart, attempting to do so without breaking any bones. They practiced pull-ups and other finger-strengthening workouts, which allowed them to hang off walls and tree branches for hours at a time. While the *shinobi* often carried out missions as solo agents, some assignments required teamwork; bearing this in mind, they practiced scaling walls and other gymnastics stunts in tandem with other ninjas to cement their synergy.

Moreover, the finest ninjas were exceptional contortionists. They grew accustomed to dislocating their joints on the fly so they could squeeze through narrow and compact spaces comfortably. They also practiced *Uzura-gakure,* which meant dropping to the ground and curling themselves into a ball in one fell swoop and remained rooted to the spot for several hours. Needless to say, the *shinobi* were peerless when it came to both bare-handed and armed combat, but because it was ingrained in them to only turn to bloodshed as a last resort, they dedicated the bulk of their training sessions to honing surprise, misdirection, self-defense, and getaway techniques, which they found to be more effective in sticky situations. Ninjas rehearsed these herculean stunts day in and day out, and continually challenged themselves to beat their own records.

Of course, physical might was only part of the equation. Mental agility was another critical component in the *shinobi* training curriculum. To sharpen their memory and focus, ninjas sat in a pitch-black room, and without moving a muscle, gazed at the flickering flame of a fresh candle until it fizzled out – sometimes, up to nine hours later. To fine-tune their hearing, they repeatedly dropped a needle onto a wooden floor, listening for the infinitesimal thud over and over again. They also practiced a special breathing pattern known as "dual breathing," which consisted of this rhythm: "inhale, exhale, exhale, inhale, exhale, inhale, inhale, exhale." Not only did this breathing style supposedly increase oxygen intake, it was also thought to help with concentration.

Unlike most other civilians brought up in rural provinces, ninjas were highly educated individuals, as one needed to be wholly literate to follow maps, read important documents, and decode cryptic ciphers. To heighten their skills of camouflage and deception, they studiously observed and parroted local dialects, greetings, and slang, and mimicked the distinctive mannerisms of the natives, so as to increase their chances of executing their missions unnoticed. Lock-picking aside, they learned the most efficient ways of restraining their opponents, an impressive selection of poison formulas, and how to gouge spy-holes into walls and other surfaces with pocket saws. They also cased target locations for trapdoors, well tunnels, and other potential escape routes well in advance.

All this laborious physical training allowed ninjas to maintain their ideal weight: roughly 130 pounds (60 kilograms), which they believed afforded them maximum agility and flexibility. They used 130-pound rice sacks as weights on a regular basis so that they could maneuver and hoist themselves up to great heights with ease. Their strict diets also enabled them to keep their bodies in tip-top shape. The *shinobi* refrained from consuming dairy, red meat, fish, and sugar-heavy foodstuffs, and instead, stuck to unmilled whole grains, potatoes, miso, mushrooms, mulberries, chestnuts, pine nuts, quail eggs, nutmeg, and wild, nutrition-rich vegetables.

Ninjas were known to pack special snacks, designed for long-term sustenance, for the road. The *Suikatsugan,* which aided with the curbing of thirst, were spherical munches roughly 9-mm in diameter, made out of plum pulp, crushed ergot, crystallized sugar, kudzu starch, licorice, and Japanese mint. Three of these was supposedly all it took to tide them over for up to 45 days. The *Kikatsugan,* or "hunger ball," which had a taste that resembled unripened bananas, consisted of buckwheat flour, rice flour, yam, carrots, licorice root, and dried chickweed, and was preserved in sake for three years. The *Hyourougan,* which served a similar purpose, was composed of glutinous rice, yams, lotus pips, and topped off with cinnamon, and reportedly bore a texture akin to dumplings.

A simpler hunger deterrent for larger crews running low on rations was a peculiar powder that was essentially a mix of white rice, pine bark, and ginseng, which was then steamed and shaped into balls, each containing 300 calories. Ninjas who popped just one of these into their mouths could stave off hunger pangs for up to three days. When ninjas exhausted their snack supplies, they subsisted on snakes, frogs, grasshoppers, and other edible insects and berries they could find in the wild.

Interestingly enough, the *shinobi* also made certain to give wide berth to beans, garlic, and other flatulence-inducing foods before embarking on missions to prevent accidental exposure.

Contrary to the romanticized depictions of ninjas in pop culture, *shinobi* attire was not limited to all-black ensembles. As undercover agents, ninjas dressed in the clothing of the parts they played, be it a monk, beggar, farmhand, merchant, servant, priest, roving musician, an enemy soldier, and so on. In fact, they never actually wore ink-black suits, not even in the nighttime, as such a hue was far too obtrusive under the moonlight. This all-black cliché most likely emerged in the 1800s, when the *shinobi* became a popular subject in Japanese art. Actors cast as ninjas in 19th century plays and other stage performances also sported black costumes for the audience's benefit to indicate their invisibility.

In reality, ninjas dyed their duds a deep shade of aegean-blue, as these pigments were a better match the grayish-blue shadows of the night, allowing their silhouettes to blend in with their surroundings more effectively. Some also wore reversible jackets called the *"haori."* These coats came in handy for those who had to make a run for it on a moment's notice, as they could make a quick costume change by simply turning them inside out.

Ninja garb was lightweight and completely form-fitting with no dangling parts, and it functioned similarly to leotards in the sense that it ensured smooth movement, with little risk of snagging their clothes on pesky protrusions. A matching head and facial covering made out of soft, breathable material, and a pair of *tabi*, which were thick, sock-like shoes with cushioned, noise-canceling soles and separate slots for their big toes, completed their outfit. Some ninjas opted to slip a *waraji* – sandals fashioned out of knotted ropes – over their *tabi* shoes for extra grip. Another footwear gadget was the *ashiko*, a companion to the *Tekagi-shuko*, which were metal bands studded with spikes on the bottom, which provided better treading on marshy grounds, slippery bridges, and rough terrain.

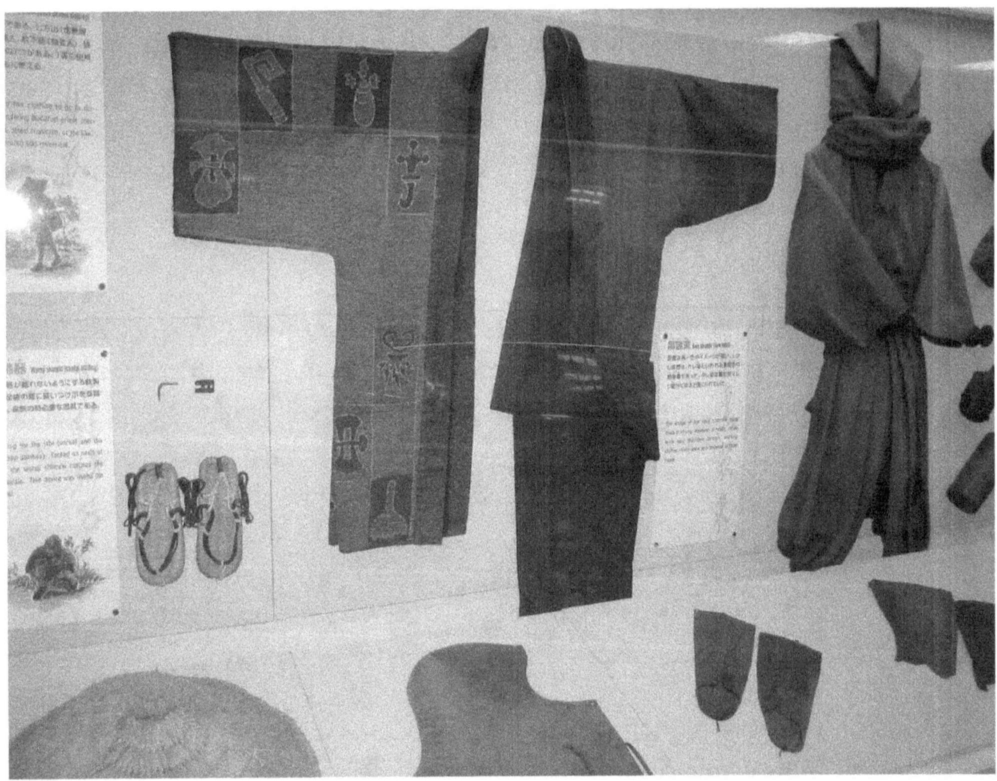

Jeremy Hall's picture of a display of ninja clothes

Sometimes, ninjas expecting close combat padded the insides of their garments with chain-mail or metal-plate armor, but most elected to forgo this extra layer of protection, as they were clunky and cumbersome, weighing anywhere between 11 and 33 pounds. After all, the *shinobi* had a penchant for invisible compartments, and the same applied to their wardrobe. The average ninja outfit was kitted out with a dozen hidden pouches, in which they stored fun-sized weapons and tools, such as *shuriken.* In addition to these pocket-sized weapons, ninjas concealed swords and arms in their leggings, and wore gloves with secret receptacles for blow darts.

The *shinobi*'s country heritage was reflected in the earliest weapons. Most of these were modified farming tools like the *tekagi* (similar to the grass-cleaving sword used by Prince Yamato Takeru), *hibashi* (fire tongs), *manto* (pruning shears), *shikoro* (saws), and the *kama* (sickles).

While it is true that later ninjas frequently fought with swords, which were stowed in scabbards slung over their shoulders, one of the most common misconceptions is that the *katana* was their weapon of choice. In truth, ninjas favored short, straight-bladed swords, as long blades with curved edges were a hindrance when it came to navigating tight spaces. Oftentimes, they slid a *tsuba* – a square-shaped appendage with a slit in its center – onto their sword handles, which, when pressed up against a wall, could be turned into a makeshift step.

The remarkable range of weapons at the *shinobi's* disposal was seemingly endless. Swords were sometimes substituted for a *kusarigama* – a small sickle with a crescent-shaped blade, paired with a lengthy chain with an iron ball or spiked weight attached to the handle. Not only was the *kusarigama* a practical stabbing utensil, its chain could also be used to trip an opponent and knock the weapon out of their hands.

A *kusarigama*

Another versatile gadget often kept in their hidden pockets was the *kunai*, a multi-purpose arrowhead that could be attached to a pole and used as a spear, and also functioned independently as a climbing or prying tool. This was essentially the *shinobi's* version of a Swiss army knife. Other useful instruments included a special compass-magnet that pointed south when placed on water, and portable pipes that allowed them to snoop on conversations in the next room.

Some ninjas chose not to use a sword at all, instead relying on firearms and explosives. The *Tanegashima,* also known as the *"hinawaju,"* was a favorite of musket-toting ninjas, which was a matchlock-configured arquebus (a European-style long rifle) that could shoot two or three bullets at a time. It was introduced to Japan via the Portuguese in the mid-16th century. Smaller pistols were also used, often disguised as short swords.

There were two types of bombs commonly used by the *shinobi*. One was a classic hard-shell, shrapnel-spewing explosive encased in iron or ceramic, such as the *Horokubiya*. The latter was a device wrapped in paper or woven wicker, then placed in lacquered, water-proof tinder boxes, which discharged toxic gas or noxious smoke upon detonation, mainly used for diversion – for instance, the *Torinoko* or the *Ibushi-ki* ("smoke pot"). Other *shinobi* bombs included exploding capsules packed with gunpowder and sharp projectiles, which were fitted onto arrows, known as the "*Okunihiya*," and the *Hyakuraiju* – a string of gunpowder-filled firecrackers.

Susan Spann, author of "Training the Ninja," discussed the prevalence of guns and incendiaries in medieval ninja culture: "Gunpowder came to Japan from China before the first European traders introduced the country to firearms, and ninjas were using explosives long before the first samurai held a gun. Fortunately for the *shinobi*, many of the ingredients required to produce explosive powders – horse dung, moxa, camphor, and even saltpeter – were in plentiful supply in the mountainous regions Japan's most important *shinobi* clans called home."

Combat munitions and survival accessories aside, a ninja's pockets were also flush with specialized trick contrivances. The *fukumibari* was a set of tiny metal pins inserted into the mouth; when pinned down and immobilized, ninjas hawked these pins at the eyes of their opponents. Some ninjas also carried a sachet of eggshells, which were emptied out and filled with blinding powder called "*metsubushi*," among other irritants. During the summer, ninjas also kept wooden boxes with cicadas or crickets inside on their persons, which was used to mask their footsteps and movements.

As the *shinobi* profession was centered on consummate discretion, it was only natural that they would have numerous methods regarding the conveyance of secret messages in their arsenal. One such method was the *Goshiki-mai*, which involved painting raw grains of rice-corn black, blue, red, yellow, or purple, each color signifying a different code, and leaving them on roadsides, next to fields, and other commonplace markers. Ninjas could create more than 100 distinctive codes based on different color combinations, as well as the number of rice-corn left on the scene. Likewise, secret notes and documents were written in code with unique characters and symbols that were only recognizable to the *shinobi*.

The *Goshiki-mai* was not the only clandestine communication method involving food. When a *genin* decided to accept a treason-related mission, they sent their *chunin* or employer a piece of salted fish. An arson-based assignment, on the other hand, called for dried fish. Different numbers, sizes, and parts of raw fish were used to indicate specific dates.

Certain pastries and sweets had their own connotations, too. Rice cakes equaled a request for extra food supplies and equipment. Those who sent sweet cakes were in need of back-up. Standby reinforcements who received bread rolls were instructed to strike rival forces from the rear.

An Immortal Legacy

"After the rain, earth hardens." – ancient Japanese proverb

At least 49 *shinobi* settlements, each with their own *ryu*, took shape in the years leading up to and throughout the Sengoku period, but there were two major-league ninja strongholds in particular that deserve the spotlight.

These strongholds belonged to none other than the Iga and Koga clans, whose domains, incidentally, shared a border. Iga turf, a completely landlocked territory, covered the north-western portion of what is now the Mie Prefecture in the Kansai region. This 215.51 sq-mi flatland was enclosed by various mountain ranges, which served as a natural defensive wall for Iga residents. Koga, otherwise known as the present-day city of Koka, was Iga's neighbor to the north – approximately 16.5 miles north, to be exact – and consisted of the southern section of the Omi Province (now Shiga Prefecture). Both these villages were seated on the Tokaido, the most bustling trade route in the empire, which linked the capital of Kyoto to Edo (now known as "Tokyo").

Iga was the archetypal, old-school agrarian community that cared little for the latest technologies and fashions – even for the time – but what they lacked in modernity and industrialization, they made up for in rolling hills, sylvan glades, twinkling streams, fruitful rice paddies, and of course, some of the country's premier ninjas. The many statues of En no Gyoja that punctuate the area today is evidence of the *Shugendo* and *shinobi*-infused culture that once prevailed in this province. Iga was also home to one of the Akame (Red Eye) 48 Waterfalls, which was christened after the red-eyed ox that Gyoja rode when he supposedly encountered Fudo-myoo, the God of Fire. It was in the ravine of Iga's Akame waterfalls that many of the local ninjas conducted their training and meditation sessions.

As Iga was just less than 37 miles away from Kyoto, it was for several centuries a haven for persona-non-gratas and refugees from the capital city, such as surviving Taira warriors from the 12th century Genpei War, who were drawn to the village's mountainous ramparts.

Some of the most well-known incomers were the scions of the infamous Mononobe Clan, an aristocratic bloodline that arose during the Kofun period. The Mononobes were hardcore Shinto conservatives who claimed to have descended from the gods. They were militantly opposed to Buddhism and vigorously campaigned for the revitalization of ultra-orthodox Shintoism and Shugendoism, in particular the ritualistic and occult aspects of these faiths. Mononobe descendants, reportedly extraordinarily talented magicians, necromancers, and seers – albeit in reality, more likely illusionists – shared their gifts with their fellow villagers. This is probably why the practices of the Iga *shinobi* were replete with supernatural undertones. Iga ninjas, for example, were known to observe the *Kuji-Goshinbo,* or *Kuji-in*, which translates to the "Nine Hand Seals": a series of hand gestures that corresponded with nine syllables that they performed whilst reciting magical protection spells.

Despite the proximity between Iga and Koga, the administrations of these provinces were significantly different. The Iga Province, then referred to as the *"Iga Sokoku Ikki,"* was a democratic, wholly independent municipality that was not in any way bound to a *daimyo*, and were determined to remain as such. The self-built governing body of the Iga comprised of a party with 50 to 60 constituents; laws, regulations, and affairs were systematically finalized by a 12-member council, hand-picked by their peers, known as the "*Iga Sokoku Ikki.*" Collectives of martial artists and former soldiers, who eventually evolved into the province's first *shinobi*, offered protection to all the villages within the Iga borders.

The Hattori, Fujibayashi, and Momochi houses were the most influential ninja families within the Iga community in the 16th century, headed by Iga Grandmasters Hattori Hanzo, Fujibayashi Nagatonokami, and Momochi Tambanokami Sandayu, respectively.

The Hattori family – whose patriarch, a former samurai trained on Mount Kurama, was the legendary swordsman that inspired the character of the same name in the Quentin Tarantino film, *Kill Bill* – presided over western Iga. The Fujibayashi family called the shots in the northeastern part of Iga. One of its descendants, Fujibayashi Yastuake, would go on to author the *Bansen-shukai,* referenced repeatedly throughout this book, on the Iga and Koga brands of *ninjutsu.* The Momochis, who helmed the largest fortress in all of Iga, ruled the roost in the southern part of the province. This formidable trinity of *shinobi* families forged a powerful allegiance, a bond that was further buttressed by generations of intermarriage.

Conversely, the Koga *ryu* was technically under the jurisdiction of the Rokkaku family, a *daimyo* samurai clan founded by Sasaki Yasutsuna of the Omi Province in the 13th century. The Kogas and the Rokkakus were tethered by a quid-pro-quo contract in which the Rokkaku pledged to abstain from intervening with Koga affairs on condition that the Rokkaku could call upon the services of the Koga warriors at any given time. That being so, the Koga Province was a semi-autonomous district, led by the Gunchu Sou family. Throughout the 14th and early 15th centuries, the stipulation within the Rokkaku-Koga pact remained untouched, and the Koga residents were largely left to their own devices. It was only towards the end of the Muromachi period that the Koka soldiers were drafted by the Rokkaku *daimyo* for the first time.

In the 1480s, Sasaki Rokkaku Takayori, having grown weary of the Ashikaga Yoshihisa's governance, incited a large-scale uprising in a bid to dethrone the shogun. He established his command post in Kannonji Castle, located in the town of Azuchi in the Shiga Prefecture, where he began to assemble his forces. Taking matters into his own hands, Yoshihisa mustered up his own troops and stormed the castle in the spring of 1487, and a bloody battle between Yoshihisa's warriors and Takayori's rebels, which included scores of Koga warriors, ensued. Takayori's men were split into two units; the main unit was tasked with fending off the shogunate's soldiers, and the other, the Koga warriors, were mobilized for guerrilla warfare.

Capitalizing on their vantage point from and familiarity with the surrounding mountains and terrain, the Koga troops descended upon Yoshihisa's soldiers from all sides, and disoriented them further with random fires and other strategic distractions. Yoshihisa's men, incapacitated and befuddled, were forced to retreat. Their attempts at retaliation over the following years were likewise foiled by Takayori's secret weapons: his Koga combatants. With Yoshihisa's sudden death in 1489, the fallen shogun's soldiers formally abandoned their campaign against the rebels. Shortly after their incontrovertible triumph, the 53 Koga families who partook in the insurgence consolidated their alliance and dubbed themselves the *Koga Gojusan Ke,* or the "53 Koga Families" – the ninjas of Koga.

Mochizuki Izumo-no-kami, who led the Koga rebels, was the founder and first chief of the *Koga Gojusan Ke*. The Mochizukis adopted the *Kuyoumon* as their family crest, which featured their surname encircled by eight full moons. Izumo-no-kami is credited with inventing the *Kemuri-no-jutsu*, or the "winding smoke screen," one of the tactics they used against Yoshihisa's soldiers. The Koga ninjas were famed for their proclivity for and mastery of logic-based, diversion ploys, as opposed to the Iga *shinobi*, who specialized in hand-to-hand combat, swords, firearms, explosives, and arson-related strategies.

Izumo-no-kami's grandson, Mochizuki Shigeie, was the captain of the Koga forces during the two Iga invasions known as the "Tensho-Iga Wars," or the *"Iga No-Run,"* perpetrated by Oda Kitabatake Nobukatsu in 1579, and by his adoptive father Oda Nobunaga in 1581 (more on these later). Shigeie also wrote *"Ninjutsu Hisho Ogiden no Kan,"* or *"The Secret Essence of the Koga-ryu Techniques,"* in 1536. The following are Shigeie's instructions to those who came into possession of these scrolls: "To our descendants do we pass down the ancient craft of incendiaries. If there is no one to pass on to, this skill will turn useless. This process is called 'Isshi Soden' (passing on knowledge to a successor). Outside of this process, it is arguable that the knowledge (of Koga secrets) can be acquired."

A contemporary portrait of Oda Nobunaga

As one might expect, this *shinobi* golden age gave rise to some of the most revered ninjas in Japanese history.

There was Kato Danzo, nicknamed the "Ninja Sorcerer," a 16th century *shinobi* who had a knack for theatrical optical illusions. Spectators were spellbound by the mage's trove of magic tricks, which included commanding flowers to blossom on the spot, and ingesting heifers and other large livestock in one swallow. It was the spectacular mission he completed for a *daimyo* named Uesugi Kenshin, however, that put him on the map.

Having heard of Danzo's astounding abilities, Kenshin summoned the sorcerer/ninja and dared him to recover his *naginata* – a pole weapon with a serrated blade – that had been stolen by one of his vassals. Unfortunately for Danzo, one of the vassal's guards caught wind of the conspiracy and proceeded to lay numerous booby traps around and within the vassal's castle, where the *naginata* was being held. Danzo's contacts warned him that the target had discovered his plans and advised him to call the whole thing off. To their dismay, Danzo was unfazed - in fact, this only emboldened him to step up his game, for he was never one to turn down a challenge.

On that fateful evening, the vassal's guards combed through every room in the fortress, and shook down every bush and tree in the vicinity, leaving no stone unturned. Unbeknownst to the guards, Danzo had already nabbed the *naginata* and had slipped up to the roof of the castle, observing their every move from afar, and was now plotting his escape. When the guards finally realized that the *naginata* was no longer in its case, they raced to the yard with their bows raised.

In the midst of the melee, Danzo hurled a life-size dummy – dressed in an outfit identical to his and attached to a rope – over the ledge. The guards were understandably disconcerted by the sight of the floating figure, but quickly composed themselves and began firing a volley of arrows at the "levitating" dummy. Imagine their bewilderment when the bandit, riddled with arrows, continued to bob up and down in midair. Taking advantage of the guards' visible confusion, Danzo tied the rope to a ridge, shimmied down the opposite wall, and fled into the night, supposedly taking one of the servant girls with him. In a different version of the events, Danzo was actually intercepted by a group of guards on his way out of the castle, but they supposedly became sidetracked when he conjured a number of dancing dolls, which materialized out of a nearby pumpkin, allowing him to hop out the window and make a clean escape.

It was from that point onward that he became known as the "Flying Danzo." Kenshin was duly amazed by Danzo's feat and rewarded him handsomely for the successful retrieval of his *naginata*. His admiration for Danzo, sadly, gradually morphed into animosity, and as a result, Danzo aligned himself with Kenshin's arch-nemesis, Takeda Shingen, who headed the aptly-named Takeda tribe in Koga Province. But again, Danzo's relationship with Shingen also soured. He accused Danzo of spying for Kenshin and had the ninja decapitated for his crime.

Then, there was Ishikawa Goemon, a *shinobi* from the Iga clan whose tragic tale and valiant accomplishments earned him the sobriquet of the "Japanese Robin Hood." Goemon was born in 1558 as Sanada Kuranoshin to a family of samurais employed by the Miyoshi clan in Iga Province. His life took a dramatic turn shortly after his 15th birthday, when his parents were murdered in front of him in cold blood, at which point he swore to exact vengeance upon the system that failed him. He found a master in Momochi Sandayu, and from then on devoted every waking moment to learning and perfecting the *ninjutsu* craft. In his early 20s, however, he fell in love with Sandayu's wife, who, to his delight, reciprocated his feelings. When Sandayu discovered their affair, Goemon was permanently banished from Iga Province.

Goemon wandered around aimlessly for a few months before settling somewhere in the Kansai region. It was here that he befriended a number of local outcasts who shared his hatred for the rich and powerful, and soon formed a crew of thieves. Goemon and his merry band of bandits spent the next 15 years robbing the wealthiest households across the region, and doled out their hearty loots of gold and jewels to random vagrants and impoverished families.

Goemon's claim to fame came in 1594, when he attempted to assassinate a prestigious daimyo named Toyotomi Hideyoshi at the newly-constructed Fushimi Castle in Kyoto. What it was exactly that triggered his abhorrence for Hideyoshi is unclear. Some say Goemon's wife fell victim to one of Hideyoshi's vicious subjugation campaigns; others say he resented Hideyoshi for the cruelty and oppression he inflicted upon the poor.

It was a pitifully piddling accident that ultimately led to the great Goemon's downfall. Just seconds after Goemon entered Hideyoshi's quarters, he lost his footing and knocked a bell off a shelf, which landed with a loud clang and immediately alerted the guards to his presence. Goemon was promptly captured, tortured, and sentenced to a horrific death. The following morning, Goemon was dragged kicking and screaming to the Sanmon Gate of the Nanzen-ji Temple, and dropped into a bubbling cauldron. Worse yet, the guards, who had abducted Goemon's five-year-old son the previous evening, forced the innocent child into the same cauldron. In some accounts, Goemon raised his son over his head as he was himself cooked alive. Fortunately, the child's cries drew the attention of passersby, who took the child from Goemon and rescued him in the nick of time. In other accounts, Goemon dunked his son into the boiling water himself, so as to spare him of what would have been a long, excruciating death.

One of the most fascinating ninjas was Mochizuki Chiyome, often referred to as the "Mother of the *Kunoichi.*" Chiyome, who lived in the Sasku district of Shimano, was a relative of Mochizuki Izumo-no-Kami and the wife of a reputable samurai surnamed Moritoki. It was only upon Moritoki's untimely death in the Fourth Battle of Kawanakajima in 1561 (in other accounts, the 1575 Battle of Nagashino) that Chiyome immersed herself in the art of *ninjutsu*. A few years later, Takeda Shingen – the same chief who had ordered Danzo's death – approached Chiyome to gauge her interest in a special assignment: to create a covert league of female *shinobi* that would subvert the activities of Koga rivals – a mission that she eagerly accepted.

Chiyome rolled up the sleeves of her kimono and went to work at once. First, she opened a halfway house in Nezu village in the Shinshu region that would function as a front for her enterprise. Outsiders were none the wiser to the goings-on of the establishment, which they presumed was a shelter for young orphaned girls, prostitutes, and women who had been rendered homeless by the various civil wars and village raids of the Sengoku period. These timid-looking women were, of course, Chiyome's recruits and Japan's first *kunoichi*. Chiyome's *kunoichi* collective reportedly boasted anywhere between 200 to 300 female ninjas at its height. These enchanting black widows impersonated bar maids, geishas, courtesans, and servants, gathering intel, stealing confidential documents, and assassinating targets.

With all that said, some historians do not believe that Chiyome actually existed, suggesting instead that her name was merely a pseudonym adopted by several different *kunoichi*. Shingen died in mid-May of 1573, though the circumstances surrounding his death are hazy. He may have been slain by a long-range sniper that had infiltrated the Takeda camp, or succumbed to wounds he sustained when his troops besieged Noda castle. Others say a bout of pneumonia killed the *daimyo*. Whatever the case, Chiyome and her *kunoichi* disappeared from all written records after Shingen's demise.

Five years later, Oda Kitabatake Nobukatsu, having recently conquered Ise Province in the Mie Prefecture, began to formulate plans for the invasion of Iga. He hired a local sympathizer named Takigawa Kazumasu to build him a fortress, later known as "Maruyama Castle," which would serve as the headquarters for the offensive operations. Little did he know, the Iga, who had always despised the hostile and short-sighted shogun-in-the-making, were well-aware of his intentions, as many of their *shinobi* were working undercover as construction workers at the very fortress. The elders of various Iga ninja tribes joined forces and on November 24, 1578, besieged the construction site and set it ablaze, reducing the nearly-completed castle to a pile of rubble and ashes.

Nobukatsu cursed the Iga ninjas for the onslaught on Maruyama Castle, and swiftly returned to the drawing board. In September of the following year, Nobukatsu marshaled 12,000 warriors and marched into Iga unannounced. Although the Iga *shinobi* were vastly outnumbered, amounting to 5,000 at most, their ferocious martial arts skills and superlative guerrilla tactics put those of Nobukatsu's largely inexperienced warriors to shame. The moment Nobukatsu's forces arrived at the valley, the ninjas diverged into multiple groups, assailing their opponents head-on and barricading all passages to hem them in.

Nobukatsu's men scuttled about in circles, desperately searching for an exit, as the skies began to rain with a torrent of flaming arrows and bullets. Meanwhile, a separate *shinobi* unit charged forth with swords and spears, stabbing and impaling any imperial soldier they could lay their hands on. By the time the smoke subsided, the bulk of Nobukatsu's soldiers were strewn across the blood-soaked grass. The few that survived the bedlam plunged their own swords into their stomachs. Nobukatsu, who watched helplessly as his men collapsed like dominoes, bolted from the scene with his tail between his legs.

Naturally, when Oda Nobunaga – the so-called "Great Unifier of Japan," who had successfully abolished the Ashikaga Shogunate and taken control of most of Honshu – learned of Nobukatsu's devastating defeat, he was livid, and vowed to finish what his son had started, but failed to accomplish. He had never cared for the *shinobi* communities. "They make no distinction between high and low, rich and poor," Nobunaga once scoffed. "Such behavior is a mystery to me, for they go as far as to make light of rank, and have no respect for high-ranking officials." Still, while Nobunaga made his distaste for the ninjas blatantly clear, he knew what these phenomenal fighters were capable of, and even berated his son for his failure to recruit these mercenaries from other provinces, whose services were openly for sale.

On October 5, 1581, in what is now known as the "Second Tensho-Iga War," Nobunaga led 50,000 warriors, many of them Koga *shinobi*, to Iga. As sensational as the skills of the Iga ninja were, this was roughly half the population of the entire Iga Province at the time. The massive imperial army spilled into the town center in five columns, torching houses and massacring men, women, and children alike. The Iga ninjas and warriors rushed to their hilltop fortress, enclosed by earthen barriers, and stood their ground for three weeks, but there was only so much they could do. They finally capitulated to the enemy soldiers and grudgingly struck a deal with the smug *daimyo*.

The Iga ninjas' harrowing defeat spelled the beginning of the end for the Iga *shinobi*. Only a few hundred escaped the bloodbath, who were consequently forced to relocate to neighboring villages to start anew. And with that, this age of sovereignty in Iga drew to a close. Numerous other provinces lost power in similar fashion in the following years, which resulted in the dissolution of multiple *shinobi* communities. Like the Iga *shinobi,* the displaced ninjas of these districts, Koga included, dispersed to safer grounds near and far, with many of them winding up in the Kii mountains. While many carried with them the wisdom and secrets of their *ryus,* as well as the hopes of establishing new *shinobi* communities, their efforts, for the most part, fell flat, and the number of ninjas stagnated.

Nobunaga died via *seppuku* in the Honno-ji Incident a year after the Second Tensho-Iga War. Immediately following Nobunaga's death, the empire descended into pandemonium as his rivals tore at each other's throats for the *daimyo*'s domains. One after another, Nobunaga's allies were vanquished, and the life of his former vassal, Tokugawa Ieyasu, who was in line to become the next shogun, was under great threat. Ieyasu's allegiance notwithstanding, a few dozen Iga survivors, headed by Hattri Hanzo, along with a number of now-homeless Koga ninjas, decided to step up to the plate. The *shinobi* fetched Ieyasu from the city of Sakai in Osaka and, utilizing shortcuts known only by the ninjas, safely escorted him to his base in Mikawa Province.

Indebted to the *shinobi*, the grateful Ieyasu welcomed them with open arms upon his ascendancy to the throne in 1603. He demonstrated his gratitude by gifting Hanzo a splendid residence within the Imperial Palace in the new capital of Edo (Tokyo). 300 Iga and Koga ninjas were also put on the palace payroll. Some were employed as watchmen, who policed the premises for intruders. Others worked as spies, posing as gardeners, housekeepers, and servants around the capital, their job being to collect intelligence regarding potential revolts and other conspiracies against the shogunate. The most highly qualified *shinobi*, specially selected by Ieyasu and Hanzo, were hired as the personal bodyguards of Ieyasu and other top-level members of the court.

In hindsight, Ieyasu's rise to power proved to be bittersweet – at least for the *shinobi*. The shogun and his successors succeeded in eliminating almost all their adversaries, and ushered in an era marked by peace and prosperity now known as the "Edo Period," which, in turn, rendered the ninja's services unnecessary. The *shinobi*, however, continued to receive employment from Ieyasu's descendants until the first half of the 1700s, whereupon they were expelled from the palace and replaced with fresh operatives recruited from the Kii Peninsula.

While the Iga ninjas virtually became extinct following Hanzo's death in 1579, the Koga *shinobi* persisted for some time, and even played instrumental roles in a few 17th century battles such as the Battle of Sekigahara (1600) and the Siege of Osaka (1614). One of, if not the final appearances of the Koga ninja – and the *shinobi* altogether – was at the Shimabara Rebellion, fought between December 17, 1637 and April 15, 1638. The Koga *shinobi* were enlisted by shogun Tokugawa Iemitsu to stamp out the Roman Catholic insurgents that had rallied round a 17-year-old rebel leader named Amakusa Shiro.

The final battle took place in Hara Castle in Hizen Province. It was there that Shiro's 37,000 rebels faced off with 200,000 imperial soldiers, among them Iemitsu's Koga ninja recruits. A passage from the diary of a Matsudaira clan member reads, "Men from Koga...who concealed their appearance would steal up to the castle very night and go inside as they pleased."

Another journal entry logged by a descendant of Koga ninja Ukai Kanemon described the espionage tactics implemented by his comrades: "[The Koga] were ordered to reconnoiter the plan of construction of Hara Castle, and surveyed the distance from the defensive moat to the *ni-no-maru*, the depth of the moat, the conditions of roads, the height of the wall, and the shape of the loopholes."

A few days into the showdown, General Matsudaira Nobutsuna, commander of the imperial troops, directed the *shinobi* to infiltrate the castle. The ninjas succeeded in this mission by cracking the passwords set by the rebels and disguising themselves as the unsuspecting insurgents. Once inside, they destroyed heaps of weapons, tools, and other supplies hidden in storerooms, and hauled off as many bags of food as they could carry. Days later, Nobutsuna mobilized a second batch of *shinobi,* who were tasked with assessing what was left of the rebels' dwindling provisions. Once again, the ninjas achieved their objective, and even managed to swipe a banner emblazoned with a Christian cross.

As the majority of their supplies had been ransacked by the imperial ninjas, the rebels subsisted on moss and castle mice. Shiro's enervated men surrendered a few days later, and the young rebel leader himself was seized and executed. The boy's head was skewered on a pike and paraded around Nagasaki, a gruesome message to all Japanese Christians.

A modern picture of the ruins of Hara Castle

At this stage, the *shinobi* were quickly becoming a bygone profession. By the late 18th century, there were only a few hundred ninjas left – if even – across the empire. Kishu Domain housed most of the remaining *shinobi*, numbering a little over 200, followed by Kishiwada and Kawagoe with 50 each, Matsue with 30, Hirosaki with 20, Fukui with 12, Hikone and Okayama with 10 each, and last, but not least, Ako, where only five ninjas remained.

Now that the ninjas were a mere shadow of the fearsome force they once were, they were reverted to ordinary civilians, each determined by their previous statuses in the *shinobi* hierarchy. Many attempted to eke out a living by becoming freelance agents, but as stated, even these project-based jobs were in increasingly short supply.

The *jonin*, who were considered part of the samurai class, fared best out of all the *shinobi*, as they transitioned into samurais, and were given dibs on the coveted positions of watchmen or fire patrol in the Imperial Palace. Although some found work as palatial spies in the late Edo period, undercover intelligence operations were soon passed on to a newly-created governmental organization called the *Oniwaban*, founded by Tokugawa Yoshimune, the precursor to the Japanese secret service. Former *chunin* segued into above-average or middling professions, mainly doctors, pharmacy proprietors, merchants, martial arts instructors, and fireworks manufacturers. Ninjas who belonged to the *genin* rank, however, were stigmatized as "untouchables," and were reduced to common thieves, street performers, and paupers. Others moved up to the mountains, where they shut themselves off from the rest of the world and lived as hermits.

By the time of the Meiji Restoration in 1868, ninjas had all but faded out of existence. Be that as it may, *shinobi* culture lived on, as they became the titular characters and protagonists in legions of fictional novels, kabuki plays, and other forms of 19th century media. These creative works, the popularity of which spread like wildfire, engendered many of the myths associated with the ninja to this day. While ninjas in literature were certainly inspired by real-life *shinobi*, writers bestowed upon them a multitude of incredible magical abilities for dramatic effect. Such powers included flight, the ability to walk on water (*Mizugomo-no-jutsu*), clairvoyance (*Sakki-jutsu*), mind control, the ability to shape-shift into objects or blend in with the background like chameleons (*Kakuremi-no-jutsu*), the ability to clone themselves (*Bunshin*), the ability to produce fire with their palms (*Katon-no-jutsu*), the ability to summon animals (*Kuchiyose*), the ability to grow up to 7-ft in height, and the ability to grow two extra heads.

The popularity of literary ninjas was propelled to even greater heights during the Taisho period (1912-1926). This resurgence was kindled by the publication of *Tachikawa Bunko,* a children's book series built around a character named Sarutobi Sasuke, an invincible ninja raised by monkeys, who went on to become the leader of the Sanada Ten Braves. It is widely believed that Sasuke was an amalgamation of Sarutobi Nisuke and Kozuki Sasuke, two real-life *shinobi.* The '50s and '60s was also something of a pop-culture *shinobi* renaissance, as this period gave rise to countless more novels such as the *Shinobi no Mono* series, by Tomoyoshi Murayama, and *Ninpo Zenshu,* by Yamada Kazetaro. Ninjas also began to grace the silver screen, as seen in *Shinobi no Mono*, based on the aforementioned book series of the same name, which spawned eight films between 1962 and 1966. The Ninja Museum of Igaryu, located near the Iga Ueno Castle, opened its doors in 1964.

Fast forward to the present day, and ninjas are as relevant as ever. In 2017, Mie University made history by establishing the first-ever international research center dedicated to the *shinobi* and the art of *ninjutsu.* The following year, the innovative institution made history again by debuting the world's first graduate master course on the subject. In 2020, Genichi Mitsuhashi, a 45-year-old dojo-owner and kung-fu expert, became the first student in the world to be awarded a master's degree in ninja studies.

One could say that the legacy of the historical *shinobi* rests on the shoulders of two individuals: 72-year-old Jinichi Kawakami and 89-year-old Masaaki Hatsumi, who are believed to be the last living ninja grandmasters. Kawakami, an engineer by day, began learning *ninjutsu* at the age of six from his *sensei* Masazo Ishida, the 21st chief of the Ban tribe, (one of the families within the *Koga Gojusan Ke*), and inherited the clan's prized scrolls on his 18th birthday. Hatsumi, allegedly one of the last living descendants of the Togakure clan, founded *Bujinkan*, an international martial arts organization with more than 300,000 members, back in 1970. Several *Bujinkan* graduates, according to Hatsumi, have gone on to become high-ranking police and military personnel around the globe. To round off his glittering career, Hatsumi was also employed as a martial arts adviser for multiple big-budget movies, one of them being the fifth James Bond installment, *You Only Live Twice* (1967).

Ultimately, both Kawakami and Hatsumi have agreed that they have no plans to appoint an heir, so it appears this most famous of age-old professions may die with them.

Online Resources

Other books about Japan by Charles River Editors

Other books about ninjas on Amazon

Bibliography

Asano, J. (2017, November 2). The Ancient Ninja Strongholds of Iga & Koka. Retrieved March 12, 2021, from https://allabout-japan.com/en/article/2079/

Broughton, C. (2018, December 5). The Greatest Ninjas In Pop Culture History. Retrieved March 12, 2021, from https://filmschoolrejects.com/most-memorable-ninjas-movies-and-tv/

Cartwright, M. (2019, June 3). Ninja. Retrieved March 12, 2021, from https://www.ancient.eu/Ninja/

Cowie, A. (2018, December 3). 300-Year-Old Ninja Master's Oath Alludes To The Secrets Of The Masked Deadly Assassins. Retrieved March 12, 2021, from https://www.ancient-origins.net/news-history-archaeology/ninja-oath-0011096

Cummins, A. (2017, June 5). Samurai, Spy, Commando: Who were the Real Ninja? Retrieved March 12, 2021, from https://brewminate.com/samurai-spy-commando-who-were-the-real-ninja/

Editors, A. N. (2011, April 26). Etymology. Retrieved March 12, 2021, from http://aboutninjas.blogspot.com/2011/04/etymology.html

Editors, A. N. (2011, April 26). Shimabara rebellion. Retrieved March 12, 2021, from http://aboutninjas.blogspot.com/2011/04/shimabara-rebellion.html

Editors, B. B. (2020, July 17). The other kind of Shinobi – Toda's Mitsumono Kamari. Retrieved March 12, 2021, from https://www.bkrbudo.com/the-other-kind-of-shinobi-todas-mitsumono-kamari/

Editors, B. E. (2015, November 6). Yamato Takeru. Retrieved March 12, 2021, from https://www.britannica.com/topic/Yamato-Takeru

Editors, E. (2016). 5 Remarkable Real Life Ninja. Retrieved March 12, 2021, from http://eskify.com/5-remarkable-real-life-ninja/

Editors, E. C. (2021, March 2). En No Gyōja. Retrieved March 12, 2021, from https://www.encyclopedia.com/environment/encyclopedias-almanacs-transcripts-and-maps/en-no-gyoja

Editors, F. D. (2016, September). NINJA STEALTH, LIFESTYLE, WEAPONS AND TRAINING. Retrieved March 12, 2021, from http://factsanddetails.com/japan/cat16/sub107/entry-5321.html

Editors, H. C. (2018, October 26). 16 Things You Didn't Know About the Origins of Ninjas. Retrieved March 12, 2021, from https://historycollection.com/16-things-you-didnt-know-about-the-origins-of-ninjas/6/

Editors, H. J. (2018, May 26). Yamato Takeru. Retrieved March 12, 2021, from https://historyofjapan.co.uk/wiki/yamato-takeru/

Editors, H. P. (2011, March 4). Hierarchy Inside the Ninja Village. Retrieved March 12, 2021, from https://discover.hubpages.com/education/Life-and-Hierarchy-in-the-Ninja-Society

Editors, I. N. (2010). What are Ninjutsu and Ninja? Retrieved March 12, 2021, from https://www.iganinja.jp/en/about/ninja.html

Editors, J. N. (2019). 1. Ninja Basics. Retrieved March 12, 2021, from https://ninja-official.com/whats-ninja?lang=en

Editors, J. P. (2019, May 6). Getting to Know Ninja, The Mysterious Warrior of Japan. Retrieved March 12, 2021, from https://jpassport.asia/media/120-getting-to-know-ninja-the-mysterious-warrior-of-japan

Editors, J. T. (2016, May 25). Discover the clandestine world of the ninja. Retrieved March 12, 2021, from https://www.japantimes.co.jp/life/2016/05/25/travel/discover-clandestine-world-ninja/

Editors, K. N. (2020). Mochizuki Izumonokami and Koka Ninja. Retrieved March 12, 2021, from https://www.kouka-ninjya.com/la_en/knowridge/

Editors, K. S. (2019, August 27). THE IGA REVOLT: THE GREATEST HISTORICAL BATTLE OF THE SHINOBI. Retrieved March 12, 2021, from https://katanasforsale.com/the-iga-revolt-the-greatest-historical-battle-of-the-shinobi/

Editors, L. C. (2017, May 23). Isshi Soden and a Page from the Koka Tradition. Retrieved

March 12, 2021, from https://lightinthecloudsblog.com/2017/05/23/isshi-soden-and-a-page-from-the-koka-tradition/

Editors, M. M. (2018). The Tale of En no Gyōja. Retrieved March 12, 2021, from https://www.metmuseum.org/art/collection/search/75736

Editors, M. T. (2017, May 3). Kunoichi: A Closer Look At The Female Ninja Spies of Old Japan. Retrieved March 12, 2021, from https://www.mysterytribune.com/kunoichi-closer-look-female-ninja-spies-old-japan/

Editors, N. A. (2008). The 18 skills of the Togakure Ryu Ninja. Retrieved March 12, 2021, from http://www.ninjutsu.org.uk/the-18-skills-of-the-togakure-ryu-ninja.html

Editors, N. E. (2015). How Ninja lives a life everyday. Retrieved March 12, 2021, from http://www.ninjaencyclopedia.com/reality/ninja-life.html

Editors, N. E. (2015). How Ninjas actually walk. Retrieved March 12, 2021, from http://www.ninjaencyclopedia.com/techniques/ninjawalk.html

Editors, N. E. (2015). Kunoichi - The Female Ninja. Retrieved March 12, 2021, from http://www.ninjaencyclopedia.com/reality/kunoichi.html

Editors, N. E. (2015). Ninja's ever-changing Costume. Retrieved March 12, 2021, from http://www.ninjaencyclopedia.com/reality/ninja-costume.html

Editors, N. E. (2015). Ninja's special food. Retrieved March 12, 2021, from http://www.ninjaencyclopedia.com/reality/ninjafood.html

Editors, N. E. (2015). The Abilities of Ninjas. Retrieved March 12, 2021, from http://www.ninjaencyclopedia.com/ninja/ability.html

Editors, N. E. (2015). The Organization of Ninja. Retrieved March 12, 2021, from http://www.ninjaencyclopedia.com/reality/ninja-organization.html

Editors, N. E. (2015). The Rule of Ninja. Retrieved March 12, 2021, from http://www.ninjaencyclopedia.com/reality/rule.html

Editors, N. E. (2015). Tricks and Traps in Ninja House. Retrieved March 12, 2021, from http://www.ninjaencyclopedia.com/reality/ninjahouse.html

Editors, N. M. (2014). "Magic and Fire", two skills of Iga-ryu Ninjutsu. Retrieved March 12, 2021, from https://www.iganinja.jp/cn/about/igaryu.html

Editors, P. E. (2019, August 2). The Japanese Robin Hood: Ishikawa Goemon. Retrieved

March 12, 2021, from https://www.peak-experience-japan.com/blog/492

Editors, S. C. (2020, June 27). Japan's first Ninja Studies graduate tried to live like a real ninja. Retrieved March 12, 2021, from https://www.scmp.com/news/asia/east-asia/article/3090830/japans-first-ninja-studies-graduate-tried-live-real-ninja

Editors, S. E. (2014, October 30). Tengu: Trick or Treat. Retrieved March 12, 2021, from http://shinobiexchange.com/tengu-trick-or-treat/

Editors, S. N. (2019). Mochizuki Chiyome | Leader of the Only Female Ninja Clan. Retrieved March 12, 2021, from https://www.swordsofnorthshire.com/mochizuki-chiyome-leader-of-only-female-ninja-clan-in-history

Editors, S. N. (2020). Ishikawa Goemon: Was he Really the Robin Hood of Japan? Retrieved March 12, 2021, from https://www.swordsofnorthshire.com/ishikawa-goemon-was-he-really-the-robin-hood-of-japan

Editors, T. (2015, August 7). THE UNIQUE WEAPONS OF ANCIENT JAPAN. Retrieved March 12, 2021, from https://www.tofugu.com/japan/ancient-japanese-weapons/#:~:text=Horokubiya%3A%20Bombs%20Away,-Source%3A%20Jiao%20Yu&text=Also%20used%20in%20naval%20combat,in%20iron%2C%20ceramics%20or%20paper.&text=According%20to%20Stephen%20Turnbull's%20Fighting,handheld%20catapults%20resembling%20lacrosse%20sticks.

Editors, T. (2018, December 14). [Exploring Ninja Village]Momochi Sandayu's fortress in Iga's Hojiro was impregnable, surely befitting the leader of ninja. Retrieved March 12, 2021, from https://www.tabido.jp/en-us/article/1327/

Editors, T. R. (2016). History of Togakure Ryu. Retrieved March 12, 2021, from http://ninjutsu.com/about-us/9-ryu-schools/togakure-ryu/

Editors, W. B. (2013, February 5). The History Of Ninjas. Retrieved March 12, 2021, from https://www.wbur.org/onpoint/2013/02/05/the-history-of-ninjas

Editors, W. L. (2015). Ninja Warrior Ranks and Classes. Retrieved March 12, 2021, from http://www.warriorsandlegends.com/japanese-warriors/ninja-warriors/ninja-warrior-ranks-and-classes/

Editors, W. L. (2017). Ninja Warrior Stealth Techniques. Retrieved March 12, 2021, from http://www.warriorsandlegends.com/japanese-warriors/ninja-warriors/ninja-warrior-stealth-techniques/

Editors, W. L. (2018). Ninja Warrior Tools. Retrieved March 12, 2021, from http://www.warriorsandlegends.com/japanese-warriors/ninja-warriors/ninja-warrior-tools/

Editors, W. N. (2009, October 27). Kato Danzo, The Ninja Illusionist. Retrieved March 12, 2021, from https://www.wayofninja.com/kato-danzo-the-ninja-illusionist/

Editors, W. P. (2019). MAN'YŌSHŪ 万葉集. Retrieved March 12, 2021, from http://www.wakapoetry.net/poems/anthologies/manyoshu-%E4%B8%87%E8%91%89%E9%9B%86/

Editors, Y. (2017, November 14). The Legendary Shimabara Rebellion. Retrieved March 12, 2021, from http://yabai.com/p/3409

Editors, Y. (2021). Teratsutsuki. Retrieved March 12, 2021, from http://yokai.com/teratsutsuki/

Editors, Y. M. (2020, April 10). Women Warriors: Mochizuki Chiyome. Retrieved March 12, 2021, from https://yamatomagazine.home.blog/2020/04/10/women-warriors-mochizuki-chiyome/

Editors, Y. M. (2020, March 11). Japan's Deadly Female Ninjas: Walking The Path Of The Kunoichi. Retrieved March 12, 2021, from https://yamatomagazine.home.blog/2020/03/11/japans-deadly-female-ninjas-walking-the-path-of-the-kunoichi/

Frost, N. (2018, May 16). The 'Ninja Diet' Prioritized Fortitude, Stealth, and Eliminating Body Odor. Retrieved March 12, 2021, from https://www.atlasobscura.com/articles/what-did-ninjas-eat

Grabianowski, E. (2004, April 14). How Ninja Work. Retrieved March 12, 2021, from https://people.howstuffworks.com/ninja5.htm

Hannah, D. (2019, June 12). Where to See Ninjas in Japan. Retrieved March 12, 2021, from https://alljapantours.com/japan/travel/where-to-go/where-are-the-ninjas-travel-japan/

Hartanto, S. S. (2017, October 7). A Guide to Ninja Weapons. Retrieved March 12, 2021, from https://taiken.co/single/a-guide-to-ninja-weapons/

Hartanto, S. S. (2019, December 2). Tengu – the Japanese God & His Cultural Impact. Retrieved March 12, 2021, from https://taiken.co/single/tengu-the-japanese-god-his-cultural-impact/

Hays, J. (2009). NINJAS IN JAPAN AND THEIR HISTORY. Retrieved March 12, 2021, from http://factsanddetails.com/japan/cat16/sub107/item498.html

Hervey, F. (2017, November 6). Togakure Ryu. Retrieved March 12, 2021, from http://ninjutsulondon.com/togakure-ryu/

Hickman, K. (2017, March 17). Tokugawa Shogunate: Shimabara Rebellion. Retrieved March 12, 2021, from https://www.thoughtco.com/tokugawa-shogunate-shimabara-rebellion-2360804

Hoshino, H. (2019, February 22). Japanese Tanegashima Musketry. Retrieved March 12, 2021, from https://medium.com/@harunakahoshino/japanese-tanegashima-musketry-2e60b1726d48

Keatinge, J. (2020, June 15). The History of Ninjas. Retrieved March 12, 2021, from https://www.samuraitours.com/the-history-of-ninjas/

Knighton, A. (2017, August 18). Japan's Onin War – A Vital Moment In The History Of Japan. Retrieved March 12, 2021, from https://www.warhistoryonline.com/medieval/the-onin-war-m.html

Lanka, L. (2008, September 7). Tengu, The Ancestors Of Ninja. Retrieved March 12, 2021, from https://www.wayofninja.com/tengu-the-ancestors-of-ninja/#:~:text=Based%20on%20Japanese%20folklore%2C%20the,half%20man%2C%20half%20crow).

Lombardi, L. (2016, November 15). TENGU: THE JAPANESE DEMON THAT'S BASICALLY A MINI-GOD. Retrieved March 12, 2021, from https://www.tofugu.com/japan/tengu/

Lucas, R. (2020). 186E. Yamato Takeru. Retrieved March 12, 2021, from https://www.rodsshinto.com/yamato-takeru

Malik, D. (2011, September 16). Origin of the word Ninja. Retrieved March 12, 2021, from https://sites.google.com/site/fsninjaacademy/martial-arts-1/originofthewordninja

Miles, K. (2014). The Correct Mind for Ninjutsu (Part 1). Retrieved March 12, 2021, from https://www.kageninjagear.com/ninja-mind-part-1/

Miles, K. (2015). The Correct Mind for Ninjutsu (Part 2). Retrieved March 12, 2021, from https://www.kageninjagear.com/ninja-mind-part-2/

Miles, K. (2018). The Most Famous Female Ninja is Revealed: Mochizuki Chiyome. Retrieved March 12, 2021, from https://www.kageninjagear.com/female-ninja-mochizuki-chiyome/

Miles, K. (2019). Kunoichi: Exploring the History of Female Ninjas. Retrieved March 12, 2021, from https://www.kageninjagear.com/kunoichi-exploring-female-ninjas/

Miles, K. (2020). The Legendary Ninja Battle of the Tensei-Iga War. Retrieved March 12, 2021, from https://www.kageninjagear.com/ninja-battle-tensei-iga-war/

Nishimura, K. (2018, January 1). The Ninja and the Kunoichi. Retrieved March 12, 2021, from https://kazukonishimura.com/2018/01/01/the-ninja-and-the-kunoichi-the-medieval-secret-service-agents/

Nuwer, R. (2012, August 21). Meet Jinichi Kawakami, Japan's Last Ninja. Retrieved March 12, 2021, from https://www.smithsonianmag.com/smart-news/meet-jinichi-kawakami-japans-last-ninja-28889515/

Oi, M. (2012, November 23). Japan's ninjas heading for extinction. Retrieved March 12, 2021, from https://www.bbc.com/news/magazine-20135674

Ozaki, Y. T. (2017). THE STORY OF PRIN YAMATO TAKE. Retrieved March 12, 2021, from https://etc.usf.edu/lit2go/72/japanese-fairy-tales/4852/the-story-of-prince-yamato-take/

Perez, Z. (2015, March 29). 4th century: The Legend of Prince Yamatotakeru: The path he took and Yamato's expansion. Retrieved March 12, 2021, from https://heritageofjapan.wordpress.com/following-the-trail-of-tumuli/4th century-the-legend-of-prince-yamatotakeru-the-path-he-took-and-yamatos-expansion/

Price, S. (2017). Mochizuki Chiyome and the Kunoichi. Retrieved March 12, 2021, from https://www.sarehprice.com/blog/mochizuki-chiyome

Riley, E. C. (2014, February 24). 10 Amazing Legends Of Ninjas From History. Retrieved March 12, 2021, from https://listverse.com/2014/02/24/10-amazing-legends-of-ninjas-from-history/

Runnebaum, A. (2016, February 22). 7 Things you didn't know about Ninja. Retrieved March 12, 2021, from https://japandaily.jp/7-things-didnt-know-ninja-2630/

Schumacher, M. (2015, May 23). Shugendo: Path to Mystic Power Via Ascetic Practices. Retrieved March 12, 2021, from https://www.onmarkproductions.com/html/shugendou.html

Serena, K. (2019, September 3). The True Story Of Hattori Hanzō: From 16th century Japan To 'Kill Bill'. Retrieved March 12, 2021, from https://allthatsinteresting.com/hattori-hanzo

Sheriff, Y. (2017). Category:Karuwaza, Acrobatics, spatial awareness - Ninjutsu. Retrieved March 12, 2021, from https://www.akban.org/wiki/Category:Karuwaza,_Acrobatics,_spatial_awareness_-_Ninjutsu

Sheriff, Y. (2017). Togakure ryu. Retrieved March 12, 2021, from https://www.akban.org/wiki/Togakure_ryu

Spann, S. (2013, June 29). Kunoichi: Female Ninja Spies of Medieval Japan. Retrieved March

12, 2021, from https://www.criminalelement.com/kunoichi-female-ninja-spies-medieval-japan-susan-spann/

Spann, S. (2014, August 28). Shinobi Shuko: The Ninja's Climbing Claws. Retrieved March 12, 2021, from http://www.susanspann.com/shinobi-shuko-the-ninjas-climbing-claws/

Spann, S. (2015, November 15). Training the Ninja. Retrieved March 12, 2021, from https://murderiseverywhere.blogspot.com/2015/11/training-ninja.html

Sunday, E. (2019, December 15). En no Ozunu. Retrieved March 12, 2021, from https://historyofjapan.co.uk/wiki/en-no-ozunu/

Szczepanski, K. (2018, August 11). The Greatest Ninja Battle in 1581. Retrieved March 12, 2021, from https://www.thoughtco.com/the-greatest-ninja-battle-195580

Szczepanski, K. (2019, July 18). The History of Japanese Ninjas. Retrieved March 12, 2021, from https://www.thoughtco.com/history-of-the-ninja-195811

Szczepanski, K. (2019, July 23). The 7 Most Famous Ninjas of Feudal Japan. Retrieved March 12, 2021, from https://www.thoughtco.com/famous-ninjas-195587

Taylor, V. L. (2016, July 25). The 3 Stages Of A Scientific Ninja Exhibition At The Miraikan (Tokyo). Retrieved March 12, 2021, from https://www.wayofninja.com/ninja-miraikan-2016/

Turnbull, S. (2015, March). The Ninja: An Invented Tradition? Retrieved March 12, 2021, from https://digitalcommons.kennesaw.edu/cgi/viewcontent.cgi?referer=https://www.google.com/&httpsredir=1&article=1161&context=jgi

Free Books by Charles River Editors

We have brand new titles available for free most days of the week. To see which of our titles are currently free, click on this link.

Discounted Books by Charles River Editors

We have titles at a discount price of just 99 cents everyday. To see which of our titles are currently 99 cents, click on this link.

www.ingramcontent.com/pod-product-compliance
Lightning Source LLC
Chambersburg PA
CBHW080853160726
47999CB00009B/3101